A Better Understanding of Coin Flipping Probability and Its Relative Outcome When Distance Is Applied

Vol. 4

Matt Fennell & Peter Porteous

ISBN: 979-8-3304-3568-5

Introduction

Harvey Dent, who spent much of his time studying probability theory, died in 2014, by his own hand. As many of you know, he was the creator of Volumes 1 through 3, and we were fortunate enough to be given the chance to supply this addition to the coin-flipping community.

We hope we were able to capture the magic of his lifelong passion for coin-flipping statistics, and the effect time and distance have on the physical outcomes. We thank his family for the opportunity granted to us and hope this Volume will help to clear up any unanswered questions remaining from the first three educational records.

"If I had a quarter for every time I became perplexed, I'd ponder, "Wherever did this quarter appear from?" Subsequently, yet another quarter would appear, leaving me to contemplate these quarters even further. Leading to still even more quarters and confoundment, until eventually I'd be slowly crushed by quarters without ever knowing why."

\-   Hrand Arakelian

PART 1

When considering possible outcomes of a coin flip, there are many variables one must reliably apply in a controlled environment in order to come to the most accurate conclusion. Conditions that a novice coin flip enthusiast might overlook such as relative humidity, lunar cycles, and menstrual activity become paramount when applied to these probable outcome calculations.

To begin our first lesson, you will need a pen, a paper pad, a young African muskrat with the ability to play darts, and a basic pocket calculator. Now if you're unable to get access to a pen, not to worry, a pencil will do.

First, let's start with a basic bitch example. You and a partner will need to map out coin flips over time. To do this, you and a partner will need to map out coin flips over time. Start with each of you flipping a coin every hour on the hour for about three and a half years. Preceding each coin flip, both you and your partner must predict the outcome. You may notice that during this exercise, one of your nipples may become tender. If this happens, you're going to need to size up your nipple against the coin. If at any moment, your nipple becomes larger or harder than the coin, stop immediately and rub one out to a slow jazz beat.

Once you've completed this coin-flipping exercise, review your notes and look for trends of multiple head or tail results. If you can't find the results, then you probably didn't take any notes. If that's the case, go ahead and repeat this exercise, this time while keeping track of each head or tail result and prediction. These results will come in handy later on, and also, they go great on spaghetti.

After finding trends of multiple correct head or tail predictions, take note of commonalities in them. Now have your partner perform the same exercise at a distance of one-thousand, five-hundred and twenty-four miles from the last coin flip. Now it's very important to understand that you won't be able to see each other. Depending on the person, this may be caused by the vast distance, or you may have gone blind due to a deficiency of vitamin A. If it's the former there's no cause for concern, if it's the latter you may want to grill up some liver and onion. Keep in mind, that your partner may be experiencing similar effects, so go ahead and grill up enough liver and onion for the both of you just in case.

We find a zesty high vinegar sauce for the liver, and a butter and garlic drizzle for the onions to be best; as garlic and onions are related and therefore complement each other on the palate quite well. You're going to want to soak the liver in milk beforehand to remove any bitterness. Then add the milk to the onions for extra bitterness. Be sure to turn the liver as little as possible as it cooks. This is done to avoid excessive buildup of acrylamide. Once the liver reaches one-hundred-and-sixty degrees Fahrenheit, remove it and allow the roasted potatoes to finish. We realize that we haven't mentioned potatoes up until this point, but that's not really all that important. What is important is that you have a proper side dish of potatoes, because potatoes were the first food ever to be grown in space. When it comes to distance, nothing is further than space (dependent on your belief system), so potatoes will get you in the right frame of mind.

Once three and a half years have again passed, and the proper distance has been maintained, we will compare the findings to one another. Take note of how often your partner chose heads or tails correctly while at distance and compare to the original exercise. By this time your liver, onions, and potatoes should be cool enough to consume. Take care not to make a mess on your notes. We've seen that mistake made before when one of us was a woman, and it rendered him with a fallopian tube obstruction. That was a painful time in his life. Once notes have been compared, you may notice that the tests reveal strikingly different results from each other, not when looking at direct matches, but when calculating percentages of correct predictions.

PART 2

As the sun rose slowly over the evergreen crested hills, a sense of calm washed over the small village of 'Scrotumberg'. I can see condensation as I exhale the cool damp air. The white fog reminiscent of the smoke that poured from my village but a day prior. If I look hard enough towards the stretch of open water, I can still make out a raft of wild ducks at the edge of the cattails. And I mean a literal raft, fastened out of wild ducks. I whack Chris's knee and point to it. Then I point to the raft.

"What!" he hollers.

It was at that moment, I realized I was writing the wrong book… let's try again.

I can see by my watch, without taking my hand from the left grip of the cycle, that it is eight-thirty in the morning. The road seems infinite as my eyes drift to the vanishing point. I need to get back to coin-flipping statistics, but I'm uncertain of my ability with my mind in such a haze. The wind, even at sixty miles an hour, is warm and humid. When it's this hot and muggy at eight-thirty, I'm wondering what it's going to be like in the afternoon. It gets me thinking about a cold beer, and maybe even a cool rag to wipe my sweaty balls. Creature comforts aside, I really just need to find somewhere to let my engine rest a bit.

Up ahead the other riders, John, and his wife Sylvia, have pulled into a roadside picnic area. Maybe we've all got a case of sweaty balls I think to myself. By the time I pull in, the others have already made their way inside. As I make my way inside, I see Jimmy Little Lips flipping a coin next to the jukebox while eyeballing me with an overly aggressive, but not too aggressive, but definitely trying to come off as aggressive, while trying to seem not too threatening, aggressive stare. I couldn't help but wonder, what the hell kind of picnic area is this!? I made my way towards Jimmy, eager to tell him about the raft of ducks I saw in the other book. Or was that this book? Yeah, it's, wait a minute... it was, or wait, yeah yeah, it was this book, but a different story.

"Jimmy, you wouldn't believe this raft of ducks I saw!"

Wham! That was a great group, also Jimmy didn't seem to care. He just stood there silently flipping his coin. Suddenly a crackling came from the jukebox speakers and a voice came through, 'Jitterbug'. The whole place broke into a fervorous dance. There wasn't much left in the world any longer besides dance. The room vibrated with energy! This was without a single doubt the most happening roadside picnic area in the Northwestern portion of Hennepin County!

Without giving any warning, I crapped my pants. I knew such behavior wouldn't be tolerated by our boss, El Culo Apestoso. Apestoso despises all forms of dancing, and he would be arriving shortly. Everyone could smell the stink in my pants, and they knew I was right. My mind jumped back to Jimmy Little Lips, flipping a coin earlier. Flipping a coin... coin flipping... distance and Kaepernick... it all seemed to add up to something.

PART 3

When distance is applied through time, it becomes four-dimensional. Now we're not really sure what that means, but it will come in handy when deciding which patterns need to be focused on, and which can be discarded. A wise man once said, "If time were as succulent as the cow's udder, one may never need goat to make pizza." We're also not sure what that means.

As three-dimensional beings, the notion of a fourth dimension is incapable of complete perception to us all. However, the fourth dimension could perhaps be thought of as the interweaving of dreams and storylines. Sometimes these dream-based storylines can be perceived as reality, sort of like if a multi-millionaire sports star was complaining that others were keeping him down. In this reality, all coin flips that will ever occur have both already occurred and are always occurring. Whether this be a coin flipped by Jimmy Little Lips or the coin flip that takes place before a kickoff. This is because the entire universe is fractal. It is ever larger, ever smaller, with no beginning and no end, kind of like the train being run on your mom right now.

If the man at the theoretical front of this train were to flip a coin, and the coin moved independently of the men in the train, then it's perceivable that the man at the theoretical end, or even the middle flipped the coin instead. This of course would be of no matter to your mother due to the limited visibility in her current position.

So, what exactly are we looking at here? Once the evidence is reviewed, and your mom moves her butt out of our face, we can see that the effect of distance on the comparable coin flips is chimerical. Indeed, the coin flip is an elusive creature. It would appear then that the greatest distance of all does not lie within the miles between the flips, but instead with the time between them. But how much time on average is between them? It's difficult to say, but we'd bet on it being close to the amount of peanut butter we use on our PB&J if the quantity of the peanut butter was formulated to represent time rather than physical volume.

In this example, the jelly would represent physical distance. Here we can see again that regardless of whether the jelly be strawberry, blueberry, cherry, sweet orange marmalade, blackberry, concord grape, red raspberry, peach pecan, cinnamon apple, gooseberry, rhubarb, or even elderberry the peanut butter will always be higher in mass.

In an experiment performed by Bollingbruck College professors in 1742, they found that when a coin was flipped at either jellied or peanut-buttered bread, 98% of 62% of the slices were peanut butter, and 77% of them were 99.9% more likely to have the coin stick headfirst than the remaining 32%, which is of course obvious. However, what's less obvious is the time taken for the coins to become fully submerged into the jelly or peanut butter. The professors conveniently happened to leave this data out of the results of this experiment. We suspect because there was a possibility of spies nearby from Argentina, working with the

Nazis to open a portal to the Peanut Butter Jelly Universe. Releasing information on how much time it takes for the submersion could have given hints to the time it would take to enter that universe. Jokes on them, however. While gathering coin flip statistics, we've irrefutably proven that the time needed to enter the Peanut Butter Jelly Universe is completely dependent on the number of soft spots in what's known as the 'Goober Medium'. Which of course, brings us to part four of our educational journey.

PART 4

Imagine if all of the fundamental elements of the universe were contained within one jar. Ironically the fundamentals can really be summed up into only two parts. However, those two parts can exist in many different forms, and in many different times. Some suitable examples being: crunchy and smooth, white and wheat, jelly and jam, or Bill Clinton and Jeffrey Epstein. Some unsuitable examples would be: tiger balm and personal lubricant, toothpaste and orange juice, or pedophiles and daycares. Now these parts cannot coexist unless they exist with additional parts as well.

You may notice additional oddities in the results of the compared coin flips that correspond not only with what we've just covered but also with additional information contained in Part 12 of 'A Better Understanding of Coin Flipping Probability and Its Relative Outcome When Distance Is Applied Vol. 2'. In this section, topics are covered on such phenomena as Simpson's paradox, and The Simpson's prediction of Trump's presidency. One of which is a gag based on an episode of The Oprah Winfrey Show, and the other is something that can be resolved when confounding variables and causal relations are appropriately addressed in statistical modeling.

Think of it this way, if two chickens lay an egg, and both eggs make a chicken, every time a chicken egg is laid, how many chicken eggs are laid when the eggs were laid by chickens born of the previously hatched eggs? That answer of course is always two. This brings us back to our jar example, where all of the fundamental elements of the universe are together and summed up into two parts. Just like a coin is summed up to two sides. That's why the cold salty air caressed my skin as I stood on the rocks looking at her boat drift and fade into the ocean fog.

I was entirely in the nude you see. A lover's quarrel always seems to extinguish like the fire that set it in motion in the first place. I could swim after her, but I have no legs, so I'd be slow and likely lose her anyway. I could trap a dolphin and ride it like a water pony, but I have no legs, so I'd be slow and likely wouldn't be able to catch a dolphin anyway. No, instead I decided it would be best to let her go. This time I would stick to the rivers and the lakes that I'm used to. I turned my back to the sea and waddled all wobbly wibbly to the old general store. I needed a job, but even more so I needed cream for a rash on my downstairs mix-up. It wasn't so much a rash as it was a friction burn. Hurt like hell either way.

As I waddled all wobbly wibbly through the front door, I immediately garnered a harsh look from the man behind the counter. We know of each other prior as I robbed him just yesterday. Our history went back much further than that, however. I wibbled cautiously towards the counter.

"Jebediah", I nodded.

He swiftly drew a pistol from beneath the counter and shot me dead on the spot.

I was like, "Not cool man."

I lurched up, drew my thirty-eight from what was left of my pantaloons, and vanished through the side wall as I delivered all six shots toward the counter. The store fell silent, and I poked my head back through the wall just far enough to see how badly I'd gotten Jebediah. Boom! Shot me dead again. I sprung right back up, dusted myself off, and flew through the ceiling into the room above the general store.

"God dammit Jeremiah!" I hear muffled from the floor below.

This was the beginning of the 'Jebediah Jeremiah Standoff'. Luckily, I had read this book before, so I knew exactly what needed to be done.

"Now Jebediah!" I hollered from up above. "You know what I done was all for that lady, I didn't mean nothin' by it towards you."

"She ain't never loved you more than my brother!" he hollered back to me.

"I am your brother!" I replied.

"A brother wouldn't have done what you did!" he snapped as he floated up into the second story.

Now staring straight at me, he lifted his pistol once more and cocked it. Haha, cocked. I closed my eyes and waited for the inevitable. I thought of my life before. Children playing on the swings in the backyard as Me and Betty sipped sweet tea on the porch, those were the days. That was before the war though. The war that took my feet, and the diarrhea took my, I mean, the diabetes took my legs. Everything changed after that, and the diarrhea, I mean depression started. I eventually fell by my own hands. That was due to the diabetes and diarrhea. I'd rather not talk about it.

"Well!?" I come out of my haze to see Jebediah staring at me impatiently. "Ain't you got nothin' to say fur yourself?" he spouts.

Then a race car crashed through the ceiling and landed right between us. It was our old pal Drivey Driverson! We both fell back amongst the wood debris and dirt.

"Drivey you dumb son of a bitch!" I hear Jebediah yell as he dusts himself off.

PART 5

Drivey climbed out of the car with a smile on his face bigger than the Adam's apple on my sister.

"I did it! I finally did it!" Drivey exclaimed, waving his hands in the air as if he did not even care. "Fuck yeah!" he continued, high-fiving both Jebediah and Myself. "I've finally figured out a better understanding of coin-flipping probability and its relative outcome when distance is applied!" he shouted.

PART 6

Now that some time has passed, you'll need to compare the outcomes from the original experiment to how they currently read. You may be astonished to find that a higher percentage of coin flip outcomes were accurately predicted than what was first calculated. You may have even guessed that llama is a funny way to spell llama. When comparing these results, we finally see what effects distance and time have played on the outcome of our coin flips.

Now with the double 'L' making a 'Y' sound, the word becomes yama. For me, this brings up memories of my llouth, when I'd ride my Llamaha LLZF up to Beartooth Cafe for their famous yasagna.

Despite their size, baby yamas can be quite dangerous. With the ability to fire poison darts from special ducts below its lower melscrocium, the baby yama is a formidable predator and has near zero patience for coin flipping. You must take great caution when coin flipping near a yama's habitat. This is of the utmost importance when conducting these exercises.

Sumtymes a yama wanna rhyde his bykickle to a chipken partang, but mostly they just chill. Most afternoons for a young yama consist of grazing the vast grasslands and making homemade pasta. With this information in mind, we do not recommend conducting any amount of coin flipping whenever you're on a grassy plane and the smell of Italian food is in the air. Speaking of Italian food, I cannot recommend enough the yasagna at Beartooth Cafe. It isn't that good, but the plates it comes on are really nice and it's worth ordering the meal just to see them.

The yamas in the southernmost western northish end near the east ends border with the westward facing part of the northern border have been known to make use of crude tools. These crude tools come in the shape of crowbars, shovels, axes, forks, hoes, plows, sickles, spades, wheelbarrows, cultivators, harrows, tractors, harvesters, knives, rakes, and seed drills. They are quite sophisticated.

The yama's mating call is unmistakable and unique to the species. While wandering mountain trails, you may hear the call of the yama, "Yama yama yo mama, fe fi fo fama, a rama rama zama, zippy zippy yay yippee yippee yippee yoo!" You should be wary when you hear this call, for the yamas are forceful maters, and have been known to tomater, or even grape their partners. They do not discriminate and often cross-species grape by luring their victims with freshly opened pudding cans.

This is perhaps due to the yama's 32% ownership of the world's largest pudding factory. Geographically, pudding is a financially stable option for the yama. The majority of the other 68% percent of the shares are rumored to belong to none other than Nicholas Oughtred, the great-great-grandson of the founder, William Jackson. The William Jackson Group's frozen Yorkshire puddings were originally created for Butlins Holiday Camps in 1974.

La gran escasez de pudín de 1986 finalmente llevó a que la especie fuera incluida en la lista de especies en peligro de extinción. Otras cosas en otras listas incluyen huevos, tareas domésticas y Bill Clinton. D'autres éléments qui peuvent ou non figurer sur les listes peuvent inclure des éléments tels que de l'eau, de l'argent, des livres ou des yeux. Pour plus d'informations, consultez la section sur le lancer de pièces avec Yamas dans Une meilleure compréhension de la probabilité de lancer des pièces et de son résultat relatif lorsque la distance est appliquée, volume un.

Now remember, coin flipping can have problematic probability problems probably produced by progressive proprietary products produced specifically for coin flipping. That's because there are like, lots of different coins, so it's hard to calibrate the darn machines properly. There was a study done near the small town of Llanfairpwllgwyngyllgogerychwyrndrobwllllantysiliogogogochuch, where they found that there are in fact a lot of different coins. For our experiments, we primarily use the American quarter, as it was one of the first pickled coins. Settlers began pickling their coins to help preserve their value. Obviously, we know now that this method didn't work, as today our money isn't worth anything. This is why we flip, to ease the pain. Of course, this type of inflation is only transitory, due to correct itself in only a couple hundred years or so.

Sometimes, if we don't have to go back to the house and replace the other one day you will get it. Boooooooy and then we will be able and get it, boooooooy, and then go out of the car and put it, a put it. That's why this final experiment must be done very carefully. Firstly, you must wear the proper personal protective equipment. Strap on those goggles, face masks, gloves, and aprons. Now to find the actual difference that distance enacts on coin flips, we need to revisit the 'Goober Medium'. This will help to overly complicate everything even further.

Simply a Newtonian gravitational potential scaler field sprinkled with fermions, the 'Goober Medium' is often perceived as several concave spreads of what appear to be arachis hypogaea with strips of what are often referred to as mesoglea, hence the name. One could imagine spreading these layers more and more thinly until you'd be able to reach the other side. Once you've reached the other side, you'd notice that the grass is in fact greener. A golfer's paradise to some, but just a place to urinate to others. However, the grass is in fact only greener due to the fact that it has had more time. A single coin flip on this side of the 'Goober Medium' can take as long as fifty-one years. Now those are dog years of course. We use dog years to measure time in the 'Goober Medium' because, just like a coin, dogs also have two sides.

Now have your partner traverse through the 'Goober Medium' and begin the next exercise. For this, they only need to complete one coin flip. When flipping opposing coins through the dog years of the 'Goober Medium', we are able to see the coin in slow motion while experiencing time that is typical to us. Divide the dog years by the number of flips obtained from flipping the coin flips that flipped from one side to the other while flipping both of the coins ten times each through the 'Goober Medium'.

After completing ten coin flips with both coins flipped from one side to the other and back, and then dividing it by seven, fifty-one times, we get 1.588656e-42, which is directly proportional to one coin flip. Take note of how many times you and your partner received both head and tail outcomes within this one coin flip.

PART 24

Have your partner return through the 'Goober Medium'. Your partner will appear much younger than you, that is of course because they are. Do not allow the flow of existential dread keep you from your research. Once all of the notes have been reviewed and the proper equations solved, and your early onset midlife crisis has calmed, you should all have come to the exact same conclusion. Distance has absolutely no effect on the outcome of coin flips, in any way, shape, or form.

PART 8

Now that you've reached this conclusion, you are finally ready to begin your educational journey. Imagine if you will, an orange with a butt. Okay good, now let's try to figure out why time has no effect on the outcome of coin flips. If an orange had a butt, what would it defecate? These are the types of questions that you need to be thinking about. Our thoughts are that it probably wouldn't at all because it's just there to look silly. Perhaps in the end it's up to the orange? Then again, is it up to a man whether or not he defecates? Let's continue to explore this topic. Cinnamon is a funny word, that might be a better topic. Saying something so bold directly to the exotic dancer you've just paid may not be the wisest choice. Doritos has a bold nacho cheese flavor, and that's something you can really get behind. In fact, Doritos is probably my favorite dancer in that whole place.

At this point in the experiment, you may have noticed I'm drunk. Also, my wife is leaving me and took the kids and my bicycle, and my house and my dog named House. He is a medical doctor you see, who solves healthcare mysteries. He also enjoys Dagwood sandwiches. I don't know what I'm going to do, I'm a ruined man. I'd do anything to get that dog back, he was like a domestic partner to me. Now writing is all I have left. "There's no living writing books about flicking quarters!" she says. My dog could talk too, and she had upsetting opinions of my literary undertakings. "It's not flicking, it's flipping!" I'd retort.

I'm here at our vacation home at the moment. I've got two cans of gasoline, a shotgun with one shell, the new album from Taylor Swift, and a bucket of ice cream. I made haste with pouring both cans onto the album and set it ablaze. I then fought fire with shotgun by shooting it with the shotgun. Once that problem was solved, I headed to the basement and tied a rope around a rafter. Obviously, there was only one thing left to do. After I was done fastening my last piñata, I grabbed my bat and blindfolded myself. Around and around, I twirled until I almost felt sick. This was the last bit of happiness I'd ever have. I headed to the garage and led a hose from the tailpipe of my car through the back window. It took quite a bit of doing, but I managed to seal off the opening to the back living room window. It was finally time to get rid of that mouse infestation once and for all. Now the time had come. There was really no other option. I made myself comfortable on one of our lawn chairs. I took a big bite from my bucket of ice cream as I listened to the hum radiating from my car's engine.

I could feel the vibration of my 1966 Ford Chevy GMC them mountains look heavy. Little boy in his yard, playing with his toy car, go buy a truck! The tabs of acid I took earlier were finally starting to kick in. I knew with the utmost certainty that I was a vampire sired in 1789 Welsh England. I suddenly had an unquenchable thirst for blood. I set out to find something to fill my tummy. It'd be a rocky road, perhaps even a mint chocolate chip. No, not this time the ice cream wouldn't do. Finally, I started to come down from the acid and realized I was a werewolf. I ran off into the night, searching for a fresh meal.

I recalled that Arby's has the meats. I began to run full speed with nothing but a classic roast beef on the mind. As a result of my meat mountain tunnel vision, I paid no attention to the crosswalk ahead; the result was to be expected. I had forgotten to depress the pedestrian button and was stopped by the authorities for J-walking.

"What do you think you're doing!?" the officer bellowed.

I had no answer because werewolves can't talk when suddenly a race car fell from the sky and crushed the police officer. It was my old pal Drivey Driverson! I fell back onto the street.

"Ruff rawrr owwooo!" I exclaimed.

Drivey Driverson drove off as if he didn't recognize his old pal, I was a werewolf after all. I quickly gave chase, I knew Drivey would want to hear what I had to tell him. My four paws smacked the asphalt with a ferocity I hadn't felt in years. Just ahead I saw Drivey pull into an old Grub Hubba Bub Bubba Hub Bubba Burgers. Now I could catch up and maybe even get myself a Double Bubba Hubba Burber Burger with extra salt.

House would have complained that a Double Hubba Burber wouldn't do my blood pressure any good, I guess she wasn't around anymore though. I finally reached the front entrance of Grub Hubba Bubs, and I broke down in tears. My favorite Double Bubba Hubba Burber Burger with extra salt was no longer on the menu. What was an acid-tripping werewolf coin-flipping theorist author supposed to do now?

Drivey came close to console me. "There there pal," he said somberly while patting my back. "You want an ice cream buddy?"

I nodded yes and gave Drivey a big hug. I felt myself changing, I was no longer a werewolf. Drivey and I sat down with our ice creams. I couldn't help but feel that Drivey's Double Bubble Mexican Sour Gherkin ice cream was better than my Bleach Ammonia Chocolate Taco. I continued eating it anyhow, I didn't want to be disrespectful.

"Drivey, I have something that you really need to hear." I handed him a demo from the hip-hop group I recently started called, 'The Bang Gangers'. "It's pretty dope, Yo".

He strapped on my Sony Walkman and started vibing. I couldn't help but smile as I choked down the last of my Bleach Ammonia Chocolate Taco; man, my throat hurt. Suddenly five and a half ninjas surrounded our table. I was paralyzed with fear, but as usual, Drivey knew exactly what to do.

"Yeah, I'll take a coffee, black." Drivey smiled at the ninjas.

I'd forgotten that Grub Hubba Bubs had their waiting staff dress up as ninjas and were equal-opportunity employers of little people. This was great because, in this town, those dirty little midgets are kind of oppressed. Mostly because they just kind of creep people out, I think.

"So, my dog left me." I finally spouted out admittedly. "Well, I mean my wife left me, and she took my dog."

"That just ain't right," said Drivey.

All of a sudden, a dinosaur burst through the window of a passing Winnebago and started charging right at us.

"Cheese and crackers!" I shouted in horror.

"What?" Drivey asked confused.

I drew my Taurus Home Defender from my sock and blasted the liopleurodon right in the giggles. The beast fell, sliding to a rest at Drivey's feet.

"What the heck yah doin' bud?" Drivey asks in bewilderment.

I glance around only to find a chocolaty ice cream spoon in my hand, and a big blue floppy sun hat on the ground. I began to feel nauseous and weak. I stumbled back and fell to the ground, knocking myself unconscious.

PART 9

I awoke, it was cold, dark, and smelled like motor oil. I could make out a faint glow of light coming through the bottom of a door on the other side of the room. I could hear the Everly Brothers playing faintly from the other side. I started to stand up, but I almost lost my balance. My head throbbed in pain. As my eyes adjusted to the darkness, I was able to see that I was hungry for pizza. I went to pull out my phone when I realized that I couldn't remember the number to Tony Tottalotino's Pizzeria and Tires Inc. More importantly, I couldn't find my really really big extra-large jumbo socks. I could have sworn I'd been wearing my really really big extra-large jumbo socks.

I just couldn't believe it. I looked in my pockets, my underwear, my socks, my wallet, my man purse, my fanny pack, my backward fanny pack, oh there I found 'em. I quickly reached inside one of my really really big extra-large jumbo socks and pulled out my handy dandy black book of phone numbers. There it was listed under "T", TOT-TINO. Then I remembered I had recently sold my cellphone for acid tabs, and now I was back to square one.

I couldn't help now but focus on the music coming from the other room. "Don't want your love anymore. Don't want your kisses that's for sure." I began to slowly make my way towards the door. Quiet like a mouse, I got on the floor and attempted to peer through the opening between the threshold and the door. All I could see was the shuffling of some old red and black high-top sneakers. The feet did creep clos'r to the doth'r. The handle beganeth to wiggle and I stumbl'd backeth in fear. I felt mine hand slip over some type of bar, haply a crowbar. The door dupp'd up and I swung with all's I had. I hath felt the crowbar maketh contact as I hath fallen backwards, the limp body falling on top of me. I did push the lad off of me and did rise to mine own feet.

I stood above the corporal agent now shocked 'I horror as I realized what I'd done. The corporal agent that lay ere me was Drivey Driverson! So, at this point, I'm like super freaked out, right? Then like, all of a sudden or whatever, a big gross nasty spider fell on me, and I was all like "Oh gag me with a spoon!" Like as if my day could get any worse. I see Drivey all like trying to move on the floor n' stuff, and I'm all like super eewww the blood is still like pleh from his head or whatever. Drivey make funny noise. Him get up and I get scared so me hit Drivey again. Bissglag Gunga grug snackleg! Porkle, "What bork foopie gragg!?" Foopie ooga arggle bruggle.

PART 9

Me skizzy whim whim. Flappa bo swangy me fleppa nippy fiz whiz? Naw dat Drivey was unable ta drive due ta his muthafn' injuries, dude was real sour towards me. I couldn't help N' therez Ain't nuthin' but feel responsible. Miff blember smezzy shweck. Once we realized the misunderstanding, me and Drivey both had a good laugh. Drivey would later change his name to Walky Walkerson due to his condition. Also, my cat Larry changed his name to Friedman.

Me and Walky decided to open a business together. 'Dog Gone It', a service for people who are tired of their dog not being able to drive them to their destinations. We'd supply specialized modifications to your typical vehicle that would allow your dog to navigate. We even had a setup for helicopters. At first, business seemed good. However, Friedman unexpectedly passed away. After a necropsy was performed, we'd learned it was cardiomyopathy that took him. Then the building burned down a few weeks after that. Walky had left a coffee & aspirin-scented candle burning after he closed up that night. We haven't spoken since.

I was pretty torn up about it at the time, but I had decided I was finally ready to patch things up. I began searching for Walky the best way I knew how. I reverted back to skills I had acquired while stalking different female celebrities in my youth. I won't mention anyone by name, but some fun random facts are that Dolly Parton doesn't have any knees and her bathroom window is almost always unlocked. She also sleeps in her makeup and has over three hundred wigs. Strangest though, is that she always leaves the toilet seat up.

I eventually found Walky in a retirement home near a beach in Alabama. I hadn't realized it, but forty years had passed and Walky Walkerson couldn't walk without walking with a walker now. That's when I first realized that I must learn how to turn back time. That's when I knew that I must find the 'Goober Medium'.

Everything that exists and ever will exist does so within the 'Goober Medium', and that is because nothing ever leaves the 'Goober Medium'. It can pull away, but the 'Goober Medium's' natural stickiness is like an elastic universe that just pulls it right back in. It's sort of like a dolphin's penis in that it can reach out and nab you when you're least expecting. This brings back a lot of repressed memories from the summer I spent as an intern at SeaWorld.

PART 12?

A man searching for answers can only question the answers to the questions he's answering questions about. This makes finding exactly where the 'Goober Medium' exists rather difficult. You always find what you're looking for in the last place you look. So, to save time I began looking in the last place I'd look. This decision would prove to have unfortunate and unintended consequences. Checking the last place first went against the natural order, which tore a hole in the 'Goober Medium'. The good part here is that now with a hole in it, it was of course much easier to find. This hole would later be referred to as 'Lacuna Magna'. Gross sure, but it's a pretty good name. I figured the best spot to check was somewhere with lots of holes (since there was a hole in the 'Goober Medium') so I first visited a Swiss cheese factory.

To receive a Grade A stamp, the eyes (holes) in Swiss cheese must be mostly between 3/8 and 13/16 of an inch in diameter. The 'Lacuna Magna' was either larger or smaller than this. Swiss cheese gets its distinctive holes, smell, texture, and flavor from three different types of bacteria mixed with cow's milk. Similar to the bacteria found in yogurt and milk, the bacteria found in Swiss cheese actually works with your body's immune system and is part of the reason why this cheese is so super yummy yummy in your tummy!

It was unclear whether or not 'Lacuna Magna' would be super yummy yummy in your tummy, but initial assessments indicated that it would most likely in fact not be super yummy yummy in your tummy. I moved on with my search and began studying episodes of SpongeBob SquarePants for more hole-related clues. As expected, the deeper I dug, the more hole I found. I couldn't help but feel like I was involved in an endless pursuit.

That's when I realized I wasn't looking at the whole hole. I remembered that I had a hole in the pocket of my old denim overalls. A hole in my pocket, denim overalls, a late-night dinner with a penguin named Deborah. It all seemed to be leading me somewhere. Back to SeaWorld! I packed my bags and headed out at once!

When I finally arrived back at SeaWorld, nobody was there. Something definitely seemed fishy, although that may have been on account of all the fish. I went straight to the Arctic Rescue exhibit and was astonished by what I saw. A group of trainers was going straight ham on an emperor penguin's red rocket. How could the penguins have possibly obtained a rocket I thought to myself. I decided to investigate further.

"Hey, how could you penguins have possibly obtained a rocket?" I inquired.

The SeaWorld trainers all scurried into the shadows as the emperor penguin turned, pointing his red rocket directly at me.

"We've been expecting you." Said the penguin.

Immediately, I recognized the voice. It was Drivey Driverson's AKA Walkey Walkerson's little brother, Smally Smallerson (different dads, different names, but that's a whole other story).

PART 11
THE STORY OF SMALLY SMALLERSON

The rain pounds against the windshield as I wait for the drop-off. Diego knows I don't like to waste my time but right now, I was the beggar, and beggars can't be choosers. It's a new moon tonight, and with my headlights off I could barely make out any of the desert landscape. I try to adjust my eyes as I see what looks to be a man cresting the top of the butte in front of me. Through the heavy rain, I can see he's holding something. Hopefully, this time he's got the right stuff, otherwise I'll be six feet under.

He continues closer as my heart starts to pound. While trying not to look frantic, I glance around at my mirrors checking for anyone else that might be around. As the figure approaches the front bumper, my anxiety peaks. My sweaty, shaky hand grasped tightly around my pistol's grape, I mean gripe, I mean grip. The figure comes to a stop in front of my car and motions me out. I cautiously open my door while I sneakily slide my gun into the back of my bell, I mean bale, I mean belt.

"Good to see you again Smally." the figure spoke with a raspy voice.

The familiar tone sets me a bit more at Easter, I mean each, I mean ease.

"Diego." I nodded.

A man of business, he takes no hesitation in opening his briefcase wide in the pouring rain. A bright red glow immediately illuminates our fascia, I mean feces, I mean faces. It looked like Diego had pulled through this time. Unfortunately for him, Jimmy Little Lips wanted no witnesses. I pulled out my pistol, put two to his chest, and his face got the rest. I grabbed the briefcase out of his hands as his body fell limp all wiggly woogly to the ground. The rain washed his blood through the mud.

Mud is created when water is mixed with dirt. Sometimes it gets all icky sticky on your shoes, like nature's dog poop, even though dog poop is nature's dog poop. Studies have revealed that dogs often poop in line with Earth's magnetic field, preferring to poop on the north-south axis while the magnetic field is under calm conditions. However, when the magnetic field is unstable, this behavior doesn't seem to occur.

This behavior is of course, completely opposite that of the yama. The yama only poops on the edges of dormant volcanos. Yet for some reason, when the volcano is actively erupting, this behavior doesn't seem to occur.

I drive off as quickly as I can, my tires sliding a bit in the mud. It was time to meet back up at Jimmy Little Lip's place and put our plan into action. By the time I get to Jimmy's, the rain had stopped, but the dark clouds still fingered, I mean lingered overhead. This is another sentence. I think to myself that this is just another prison sentence for me. I can hear the music booming from inside Jimmy's place. I walk inside and see Jimmy Little Lips flipping a coin next to the jukebox. The familiar smell of peanut butter fills the air. He smirks at me as he turns down the music.

"You eh uh, I mean like, you know get the job done and stuff?" he asks.

"I think you'll be happy this time," I reply. "Do you have the payment?"

"You'll ah get paid when the jobs is done!" He snaps. "Now let's uh, sees it." he motions towards the briefcase.

"Not until I see it!" I demand.

Jimmy Little Lips stood silent for a while, staring me right in the pies, I mean eyes.

"Alright then, ok. Well, open 'er up," he says smugly.

I place the briefcase on the counter and cautiously begin undoing the latches. I step back and gesture towards the case, deciding to let Jimmy Little Lips open it himself. The same red glow from before creeps across his face as he opens it up. Like a shiny hot dog sticking out of a wool sock, the red rocket beams with an intensity that could only be described as pretty neat.

"This. This is what I'm talkin' about here!" Jimmy smiles with glee.

Jimmy throws me a set of keys and points to the back door. I hurry through to find a beautiful Llamaha LLZF just waiting for me to hop on. I immediately go to start it up, but Jimmy stops me.

"Hey real quick like now. Look it, I got another job for yous."

"No more jobs," I tell Jimmy. "I'm gonna go start me a pickle farm in New Jersey with my brother's girlfriend."

I start my Llamaha and ride off into the sunset all dramatic-like. I promptly turn around however after realizing that I don't know a thing about pickles, I don't have any money, and I don't know where New Jersey is.

"Alright, Jimmy what is it?" I call out as I come to a stop.

"What?!" Jimmy calls back.

I'm about one hundred and sixty feet away at this point, and my Llamaha doesn't have reverse.

"What's the job?!" I yell half out of breath as I push my Llamaha back up the street.

Jimmy doesn't say a thing though, he just tosses me a duffle bag and walks away.

I open up the duffel bag and yell, "Holey begiggers! This bag is full of rattlesnakes!" because the bag is full of rattlesnakes!

I zip up the duffle bag faster than green grass through a goose. I throw it over my shoulder and hop on my Llamaha, I know exactly where to go. By the time I reach the playground, it's filled with kids. Jimmy is going to be pleased with the outcome. I scratch the words 'Free Candy' into the sides of an old panel van in the parking lot. I then stash my Llamaha behind a bush and wait. It's not long before I forget what I'm waiting for and wander off like an unattended child. That's when I met Maxwell Digerno Dibobga Dibanga the third.

PART 12
THE STORY OF MAXWELL DIGERNO DIBOBGA DIBANGA THE THIRD

Maxwell Digerno Dibobga Dibanga the third was born on Devember 38th in the back seat of a taxi in Chicago. His mother left before he was born, and his father was in and out of jail constantly during Maxwell's childhood. Luckily due to progeria, his childhood didn't last long, at least it didn't seem that way. Maxwell would later meet Smally near a playground in Albuquerque New Mexico.

"I knew I should have turned left at Albuquerque," said Maxwell as he arrived in Albuquerque.

Albuquerque spells gullible backward, minus the 'S'.

"Hey, tiger." Maxwell nodded at me. "What yah doin' with that their panel van?"

Smally knew what Maxwell really meant by that seemingly inconspicuous question. Not much gets by Smally Smallerson. Sometimes I like to think in the third person.

"I'm going to need your help getting these kids into the van." I confided in Maxwell.

Maxwell seemed eager to help and turned out to be a very quick learner. After about two or nine years, he was pretty much running the entire operation on his own.

Now that we had a van full of children, and a duffle bag full of partially alive aging rattlesnakes, Maxwell and I headed off to SeaWorld to put the plan into action. We arrived at night and pulled up at the back gate. Maxwell strapped the children with explosives while I fastened a rope out of the snakes. It was at about this time that I realized I was super hungry.

There'd be time for a quick stop at Grub Hubba Bub Bubba Hub Bubba Burgers I thought. Grub Hubba Bub Bubba Hub Bubba Burgers was me and my brother's favorite place to eat growing up, and the place brings a smile to my face still to this day. I had a decision to make, and fast. Either break into SeaWorld and steal 'Dolphin the sea lion' and 'Narwhal the orca' right this moment, or go get a Rubba Hubba Hubba Bubba Burber Burger from Grub Hubba Bub Bubba Hub Bubba Burgers.

My stomach rumbled with the ferocity of a thousand thunderstorms, and I knew I needed a Rubba Hubba Hubba Bubba Burber Burger from

Grub Hubba Bub Bubba Hub Bubba Burgers right then. Sometimes Grub Hubba Bub Bubba Hub Bubba Burgers can be a real mouthful, so I like to shorten it by just saying 'GH' followed by a double 'B' and then after that there's an 'H', and then subsequently another double 'B'. By the time we had made it to 'GH' followed by a double 'B' and then after that there's an 'H', and then subsequently another double 'B', the moon had collided with the earth causing milk prices to double. And that's not all, because firetrucks turned into wolverines, and they couldn't figure out how to swim to the island of misfit toys. But just wait, there's more. A large group of financially troubled Saudi Arabians had recently learned how to whistle, but then they'd forgotten their swimsuits. When without warning everyone's footwear teleported to a rocket ship headed straight for the sun.

Once we arrived back at SeaWorld, all of those other situations had worked themselves out. Now it was time to gain access, so we could deliver our red rocket to the penguins. I tied the rope of snakes to one of the smaller children and hucked him over the gate. I pulled tightly on the snake rope until the child became wedged between the finials, like some sort of adolescent grappling hook. Then he climbed over that fence ever so greatly on the snake rope. Well, the fact you're on the end, you made it; I made it to the other side. It was no problem. He have no problems doing it, man. I got there when I got to the other side. If he didn't deliver the red rocket in time, he was gonna blow up my car!

At this point in the story, you may have realized I'm drunk. I had gotten so nervous about the break-in that I'd downed like eight or nine pitchers of Bubba's Hubbarita at 'GH' followed by a double 'B' and then after that, there's an 'H', and then subsequently another double 'B'.

Somehow, we made it inside. I don't really remember much, but soon enough I was all dressed up as a penguin and ready to deliver my red rocket to the other penguins. The plan was coming together perfectly, I think, maybe, I can't really remember.

"Maxwell, stay behind with the kids," I whispered.

I waddled casually over to the other penguins, none of them suspected a thing. I presented them with the red rocket and they handed me the bag of cash. All of a sudden, some guy tripping on acid who thought he was a werewolf runs up out of nowhere and he's all, "Hey, how could you penguins have possibly obtained a rocket?" Even though he came out of nowhere, I knew he'd be there.

"We've been expecting you," I said, all ominous and sic AF.

The SeaWorld trainers all scurried into the shadows. The strange man seemed to recognize my voice somehow.

"It's you. I know it's you." I muttered.

The emperor penguin said nothing and just motioned someone over from the dark hall behind him. Or wait a minute... that's not what happened, hang on, I'm confused. Let me gather my thoughts.

Maxwell and the explosive-clad children gathered around me, the strange man's face turned pale.

"So, you know who I am?" I questioned.

"I know that voice," the strange man replied. "Years back I was calculating coin-flipping statistics and how the outcome was affected by distance, but in order to do so, I had to send a friend through the 'Goober Medium'."

I suddenly realized what all of this was. The penguin, the red rocket, the children wrapped in explosives. The universe was speaking to me. The 'Goober Medium' was speaking to me. It was me the whole time, I thought to myself as if the inner walls of my own mind were crashing in. Murdering Diego in the desert, the Llamaha, the duffle bag full of rattlesnakes, the old panel van, all of those Hubbaritas… it was me the whole time. Jebediah and Jeremiah, Jimmy Little Lips, Chris's knee, John and his wife Sylvia, El Culo Apestoso, your mom, Drivey Driverson aka Walky Walkerson, Maxwell Digerno Dibobga Dibanga the third, they were all just me. I felt a sense of calm wash over me.

I couldn't waste any more time. I gathered up the explosive-strapped children and the penguins and tied them to the red rocket faster than a knife fight in a phone booth. When suddenly a race car fell from the sky and crushed the strange man. It was my brother, Walky Walkerson! Although now it's Drivey Driverson because he's back in his race car, but also maybe it was just me?

"None of this makes any sense!" I cried out loud.

It's as if these cars are falling through a hole that doesn't exist yet, and time keeps skipping like a record player. I did what any man would do in that situation. I grabbed hold of Drivey and kissed him like his brother ain't never kissed him before. Suddenly the explosive child and penguin-covered red rocket ignited as if the heat from our brother passion caused the sparks that I felt in my heart to come alive. The penguins immediately started to defecate as the rocket whizzed higher and higher into the night sky.

The rocket reached what should have been the beginning of space, but instead crashed through the firmament (turns out flat earthers were right). Peanut butter and jelly started pouring through the gigantic hole in equal amounts. The rocket must have hit a soft spot in the 'Goober Medium'. For the first time in mankind's history, we had just made contact with the Peanut Butter Jelly Universe. It was absolutely beautiful!

Now that I was able to turn back time, I was finally allowed to reunite with the younger version of my old pal and brother Walky Walkerson, and properly forgive him for burning down 'Dog Gone It' headquarters. Then I thought for a bit. If I have the ability to reverse time through the 'Goober Medium', then I'll just go all the way back to the beginning!

 **PART 13**

"Push!" I can hear, but I can't see anything. "Breathe, breathe, push!" As I started to come to, I realized I had gone too far back. Back when I was an Olympic bodybuilder, and I had those pumped-up arms from lifting thousand-pound bars. Yeah, I had the biggest muscles man I had it going on. I'm not a nice dude. I'll give you bad dreams. I'll run you over if you're talkin' bout the bad things. California starts with the letter 'C'.

Beefy beefy stew, beefy beefy stew. I like beefy stew, beefy beefy stew. You need to consume a lot of protein in order to maintain a bodybuilder's physique. Beefy beefy stew is a delicious meal option to consider for this. Where am I going with this? I don't think this story is going the way any of us expected. I needed to tie up some loose ends. I really needed to get back to coin-flipping. Easier said than done, or easier written, in this case.

I wiped off my chocolate banana protein shake mustache and headed back to the 'Goober Medium'. I'd gone too far, and I needed to go back,

back to the future. I did the stuff I needed to do, and also some other stuff I'd been wanting to do, and also some stuff I'd been meaning to do. Finally, I was exactly where I needed to be.

I could smell the scent of burning coffee and aspirin as I stared reminiscently at what was left of 'Dog Gone It'. The building was still smoldering, and I knew where Walky would be on this night. I finally arrived at 'GH' followed by a double 'B' and then after that, there's an 'H', and then subsequently another double 'B' around ten thirty. Just as I'd expected, there was Walky, sitting all alone in his favorite parking lot pothole.

"You did it. You finally did it." Walky turned towards me with a somewhat somber smile. "You've finally figured out a better understanding of coin-flipping probability and its relative outcome when distance is applied!

When suddenly a race car fell from the sky, crushing us both, and killing us instantly.

StarTribun

Monday, August 27, 1979

Race car falls from sky killin

In a startling find Sunday night at a Grub Hubba Bub's parking lot, two men were killed when a race car fell from the sky in east Marshall County around 10:40 p.m. The Sheriff's Office said in a news release that the two men were crushed when the vehicle fell from what seemed to be out of nowhere. A nearby witness reported, "I don't know what happened. There was a car, and it fell." The identity of the two victims have yet to be released.

About The Authors

Peter and Matt grew up in separate households, under the same roof, in two different countries, while sharing the same time zone. They first met when Matt was five, Peter was four, and Matt was nine.

Writers, historians, and activists are all things they'd like to be. Possibly authoring over sixteen books between the two of them, on potential subjects such as: crafting, obstetrics, money marketing, lobbying, and Catholicism.

Once pardoned for war crimes by Ronald Reagan, the two would go on to accomplish a wide array of animal abuse for entertainment purposes. This unfortunately came to an abrupt end in 1992.

Once the Federal Republic of Yugoslavia was formed, the local culture began to take on a dislike towards animal cruelty. This left the two without an outlet for their simple interests and fiery passions.

Eventually, the two would wander the world, searching for purpose in their lives. In 1999 the two discovered a way to use corn dextrin as a substitute for rocket fuel, and in doing so were able to France, I mean fiancé, I mean finance their own literary undertakings.